C000111882

The Light in the Heart

Inspirational Thoughts for Living Your Best Life

Roy T. Bennett

ISBN: 978-0987917768

INTRODUCTION

I wrote this book because I want to help you live your best life. I will spread the light in my heart to touch the lives of others and make a positive impact to the world for its betterment.

One good thought that is empowering and motivating to you can change your entire life.

It's important that what thoughts you are feeding into your mind because your thoughts create your belief and experiences. You have positive thoughts and you have negative ones too. Nurture your mind with positive thoughts: kindness, empathy, compassion, peace, love, joy, humility, generosity, etc. The more you feed your mind with positive thoughts, the more you can attract great things into your life.

We might all be here to help each other. We are all gifted with abilities to make a positive difference to other people's lives. To make a positive difference is an incredible feeling and it is completely within our grasp. When I share my positive thoughts, I get a sense of happiness, fulfillment and purpose.

* The electronic version of this printed book has been published on February 25, 2016.

TABLE OF CONTENTS

Live Life to the Fullest A

Be brave enough to live the life of your dreams according to your vision and purpose instead of the expectations and opinions of others.

We have to be honest about what we want and take risks rather than lie to ourselves and make excuses to stay in our comfort zone.

It's only after you've stepped out of your comfort zone that you begin to change, grow, and transform.

Surround yourself with people who believe in your dreams, encourage your ideas, support your ambitions, and bring out the best in you.

Your hardest times often lead to the greatest moments of your life. Keep going. Tough situations build strong people in the end.

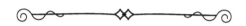

When you start living the life of your dreams, there will always be obstacles, doubters, mistakes and setbacks along the way. But with hard work, perseverance and self-belief there is no limit to what you can achieve.

Make Peace with Yourself before You Move Forward

Accept yourself, love yourself, and keep moving forward. If you want to fly, you have to give up what weighs you down. Make peace with yourself before you move forward.

Be grateful for what you already have while you pursue your goals. If you aren't grateful for what you already have, what makes you think you would be happy with more.

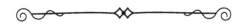

Do not let the memories of your past limit the potential of your future. There are no limits to what you can achieve on your journey through life, except in your mind.

Acts of
Kindness

A random act of
kindness, no matter
how small, can make a
tremendous impact on
someone else's life.

Help others without any reason and give without the expectation of receiving anything in return.

Stop Judging People

We are all different.
Don't judge, understand
instead.

Kindness is not a business. True kindness expects nothing in return and should never act with conditions.

Treat everyone with politeness and kindness, not because they are nice, but because you are.

Learn to light a candle in the darkest moments of someone's life. Be the light that helps others see; it is what gives life its deepest significance.

Always find
opportunities to make
someone smile, and to
offer random acts of
kindness in everyday life.

Always Help
Someone

Always have a willing hand to help someone, you might be the only one that does.

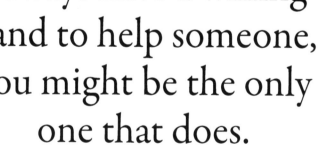

See the Good in Other People

Life becomes easier and more beautiful when we can see the good in other people.

When you start giving, instead of getting, you make a difference. You can always give a warm smile, a sincere hello, a positive vibe... your attention, your time, your love, and kindness to those around you.

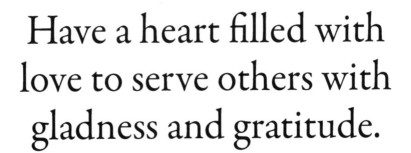

Have a heart filled with love to serve others with gladness and gratitude.

Kindness Reflects Who You Are

Kindness reflects who you are. If you are kind, you can share with the world your kindness. It is who you are, not what you do.

The More You Give the More You Can Give

The more you give, the more you can give.

If you have kindness in your heart, you offer acts of kindness to touch the hearts of others wherever you go—whether they are random or planned. Kindness becomes a way of life.

I admire those who do good and expect nothing in return. Do good, live in the most positive and joyful way possible every day.

Good People Bring out the Best in Other People

Good people see the good and bring out the best in other people.

You don't have to like someone, but you have to treat them as you wish to be treated.

Sometimes all a person wants is an empathetic ear; all he or she needs is to talk it out. Just offering a listening ear and an understanding heart for his or her suffering can be a big comfort.

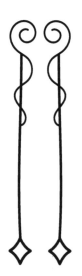

Focus on the Positive

It's important that what thoughts you are feeding into your mind because your thoughts create your belief and experiences. You have positive thoughts and you have negative ones too. Nurture your mind with positive thoughts: kindness, empathy, compassion, peace, love, joy, humility, generosity, etc. The more you feed your mind with positive thoughts, the more you can attract great things into your life.

Instead of worrying about
what you cannot control,
shift your energy to what
you can create.

Discipline your mind
to see the good in every
situation and look on the
best side of every event.

Whenever something bad happens, keep calm, take a few deep breaths and shift the focus to something positive.

Associate yourself with people who think positively. You cannot surround yourself with negative people and expect positive outcomes.

Good things happen
in your life when you
surround yourself with
positive people.

Distance yourself from negative people who try to lower your motivation and decrease your ambition. Create space for positive people to come into your life. Surround yourself with positive people who believe in your dreams, encourage your ideas, support your ambitions, and bring out the best in you.

Sometimes you have to remove certain people out of your life to make room for better people. Respect yourself enough to remove negative and toxic people from your life.

Nobody is exempt from the trials of life, but everyone can always find something positive in everything even in the worst of times.

Shift the Negative Thought into a Positive One

Instead of worrying about what could go wrong, change your thoughts to what could go right. When you change the negative thought into a positive one, it eliminates the negative one.

You cannot control what happens to you, but you can control the way you think about all the events. You always have a choice. You can choose to face them with a positive mental attitude.

Learning to distance yourself from all the negativity is one of the greatest lessons to achieve inner peace.

A Negative Mind Will Never Give You a Positive Life

Be careful the stories you're telling yourself about your current circumstances; a head full of negative thoughts has no space for positive ones. Do not let your negative thoughts have power over you because those thoughts will end up controlling your life. No one can live a positive life with a negative mind. We all have negative thoughts now and then, but we can choose not to dwell there and not to let them control us.

Start Each Day with a
Positive Thought

Start each day with a positive thought and a grateful heart.

Be Positive Be True
Be Kind

Be positive.
Be true.
Be kind.

The value of surrounding yourself with positive people is not what you get from them, but how good a person you have become because of them.

Follow Your Heart

Follow your heart, listen to your inner voice, stop caring about what others think. To stop caring about what others think is often easier said than done. It becomes easy when you can listen to your inner voice to form a strong conviction and self-confidence.

You are unique; always be yourself. The world will benefit the most from your uniqueness. To shine your brightest light is to be who you truly are.

To care about your outward appearance is important, but what is more important is to have a beautiful soul. The outward beauty will fade with time, but a beautiful soul will always be a beautiful soul.

Believe in your heart that
you're meant to live a life
full of passion, purpose,
magic and miracles.

Know Who You Truly Are

If you don't know who you truly are, you'll never know what you really want.

Don't Forget Who You Are

Do not let the roles you play in life make you forget who you are.

You will never follow your own inner voice until you clear up the doubts in your mind.

Sometimes you have to
lose all you have to find
out who you truly are.

You are not rich until you have a rich heart. A rich heart is more precious than any worldly possession; it is what makes a person truly rich.

Pursue what catches your heart, not what catches your eyes.

You attract who you are being. When you work at being the type of person that you want to attract, you attract those kinds of people into your life.

It's worth making time to find the things that really stir your soul. That's what makes you really feel alive. You have to say 'no' to other things you're used to, and do it with all your heart.

The essence of life does not consist in the abundance of your possessions, but in the richness of your heart.

What seeds you plant in
your heart is what you reap
in your life. Plant the seeds
of love, joy, peace, hope,
kindness, and faith.

The Power of Choice

Attitude is everything. Change your attitude and you change your life. You cannot control what happens to you in your life, but you can always control how you respond to it. The way you choose to respond is a reflection of your attitude. By changing your attitude, you change your perspective and change your life.

Choose Wisely

Attitude is a choice. Happiness is a choice. Optimism is a choice. Kindness is a choice. Giving is a choice. Respect is a choice. Whatever choice you make makes you. Choose wisely.

Guard well your thoughts when alone and your words when accompanied.

Every Choice Comes with a Consequence

Every choice comes with a consequence. Once you make a choice, you must accept responsibility. You cannot escape the consequences of your choices, whether you like them or not.

You cannot control the behavior of others, but you can always choose how you respond to it.

Take Control of Your Attitude

When you take control
of your attitude, you take
control of your life.

Your attitude is always within your control; there are lots of things in life you have no control over, but your attitude about any state or condition is 100 percent within your power to choose. Always choose to have a great attitude.

Beliefs are choices. First you choose your beliefs. Then your beliefs affect your choices.

Your beliefs affect your choices. Your choices shape your actions. Your actions determine your results. The future you create depends upon the choices you make and the actions you take today.

The Master of Your Own Destiny

You are not the victim of the world, but rather the master of your own destiny. It is your choices and decisions that determine your destiny.

The more you can have control over your ego rather than let it run amuck, the more successful you'll be in all areas of life.

Live Life to the Fullest B

Don't let the expectations
and opinions of other people
affect your decisions. It's
your life, not theirs. Do
what matters most to you;
do what makes you feel alive
and happy. Don't let the
expectations and ideas of
others limit who you are. If
you let others tell you who
you are, you are living their
reality — not yours.

There is more to life than pleasing people. There is much more to life than following others' prescribed path. There is so much more to life than what you experience right now.

You need to decide who you are for yourself. Become a whole being. Adventure.

**Make the Most of
Your Life and Live It to
the Fullest**

Each day brings new opportunities, allowing you to constantly live with love—be there for others—bring a little light into someone's day. Be grateful and live each day to the fullest.

**Make the Most of
the Best and the
Best of the Worst**

Make the most of the best and the best of the worst, and keep your standards high. Never settle for anything less than you deserve or are capable of achieving.

Enjoy every step
you take. If you're
curious, there is always
something new to
be discovered in the
backdrop of your daily
life.

Life is about accepting the challenges along the way, choosing to keep moving forward, and savoring the journey.

Believe in Your Infinite Potential

Believe in your infinite potential. Your only limitations are those you set upon yourself.

Believe in yourself, your abilities and your own potential. Never let self-doubt hold you captive. You are worthy of all that you dream of and hope for.

Believe in yourself. You are braver than you think, more talented than you know, and capable of more than you imagine.

The more you believed in yourself, the more you could trust yourself. The more you trust yourself, the less you compare yourself to others.

Don't let others tell you what you can't do. Don't let the limitations of others limit your vision. If you can remove your self-doubt and believe in yourself, you can achieve what you never thought possible.

There are some values that you should never compromise on to stay true to yourself; you have to be brave to stand up for what you truly believe in even if you stand alone.

Your core values act like your internal compass which navigates the course of your life. If you compromise your core values, you go nowhere.

Be brave to stand for what you believe in even if you stand alone.

If you believe very strongly in something, stand up and fight for it.

You Do Not Have to Do What Everyone Else Is Doing

You are unique. You have different talents and abilities. You don't have to always follow in the footsteps of others. And most important, you should always remind yourself that you don't have to do what everyone else is doing and have a responsibility to develop the talents you have been given.

It's your life; you
don't need someone's
permission to live the
life you want. Be brave
to live from your heart.

Create a vision for the life you really want and then work relentlessly towards making it a reality.

Dream your own dreams, achieve your own goals. Your journey is your own and unique.

Don't be pushed around
by the fears in your
mind. Be led by the
dreams in your heart.

Push your boundaries
beyond the ordinary;
be that "extra" in
"extraordinary."

You can learn to run if you walk on the well-beaten path, but you can fly if you are brave enough to travel the unbeaten one.

The comfort zone is a psychological state in which one feels familiar, safe, at ease, and secure.

Great Things Never Come from Comfort Zones

If you always do what is easy and choose the path of least resistance, you never step outside your comfort zone. Great things don't come from comfort zones.

You never change your life until you step out of your comfort zone; change begins at the end of your comfort zone.

It's only after you've stepped out of your comfort zone that you begin to change, grow, and transform.

Real change is difficult at the beginning, but gorgeous at the end. Change begins the moment you get the courage and step outside your comfort zone; change begins at the end of your comfort zone.

Real change is difficult at the beginning. Without the familiar to rely upon, you may not in as much command as you had once been. When things are not going your way, you will start doubting yourself. Stay positive, keep the faith, and keep moving forward—your breakthrough may be just around the corner.

Change is a process that takes time and commitment, not an event.

Changing your outside
world cannot make
you happy if you are an
unhappy person. The
real personal change
can only happen from
the inside out. If you
firstly create the change
within yourself, you can
turn your life around.

Change may not always bring growth, but there is no growth without change.

You are the only one who can change your life. No one else can do it for you. It's never too late to change your life for the better. You don't have to take huge steps to change your life. Making even the smallest changes to your daily routine can make a big difference to your life.

Be the Reason
Someone Changes

You cannot change anyone, but you can be the reason someone changes.

It Takes Sunshine and Rain to Make a Rainbow

There would be no rainbows without sunshine and rain.

Be the kind of the person who dares to face life's challenges and overcome them rather than dodging them.

Every challenge you
face today makes you
stronger tomorrow.
The challenge of life is
intended to make you
better, not bitter.

When things do not
go your way, remember
that every challenge—
every adversity—
contains within it the
seeds of opportunity
and growth.

Challenge and adversity are meant to help you know who you are. Storms hit your weakness, but unlock your true strength.

Difficulties and adversities viciously force all their might on us and cause us to fall apart, but they are necessary elements of individual growth and reveal our true potential. We have got to endure and overcome them, and move forward. Never lose hope. Storms make people stronger and never last forever.

Finding the Lesson behind Every Adversity

Finding the lesson behind every adversity will be the one important thing that helps get you through it.

Life teaches us the right path is rarely the easy one.

Never let hard lessons harden your heart; the hard lessons of life are meant to make you better, not bitter.

You have the power
within you to rise above
your difficult situations
and transform into the
best version of yourself.

Accepting personal responsibility for your life frees you from outside influences— increases your self-esteem—boosts confidence in your ability to decisions— and ultimately leads to achieve success in life.

The past is a place of reference, not a place of residence; the past is a place of learning, not a place of living.

Once you realize you deserve a bright future, letting go of your dark past is the best choice you will ever make.

Time doesn't heal emotional pain; you need to learn how to let go.

Stop giving other people the power to control your happiness, your mind, and your life. If you don't take control of yourself and your own life, someone else is bound to try.

What other people think and say about you is none of your business. The most destructive thing you would ever do is to believe someone else's opinion of you. You have to stop letting other people's opinions control you.

You were not born on earth to please anyone; you have to live life to express yourself, not to impress someone. Don't pretend to be someone you're not, and never lose yourself in search of other people's acceptance and approval.

Life is short. Focus on what really matters most. You have to change your priorities over time.

Practice an Attitude of Gratitude

Gratitude builds a bridge to abundance.

Has a Grateful Heart

When one has a grateful heart, life is so beautiful.

Be thankful for everything that happens in your life; it's all an experience.

Being grateful
does not mean
that everything is
necessarily good. It
just means that you
can accept it as a gift.

Everyone enjoys being acknowledged and appreciated. Sometimes even the simplest act of gratitude can change someone's entire day. Take the time to recognize and value the people around you and appreciate those who make a difference in your lives.

Everyone you meet is
a part of your journey,
but not all of them
are meant to stay
in your life. Some
people are just passing
through to bring you
gifts; either they're
blessings or lessons.

We don't truly appreciate what we have until it's gone. We don't really appreciate something until we have experienced some events. Be grateful for what you have now, and nothing should be taken for granted.

Count your
blessings, not your
problems. Count
your own blessings,
not someone else's.
Remember that
jealousy is when you
count someone else's
blessings instead of
your own.

More smiling,
less worrying.

More compassion,
less judgment.

More blessed,
less stressed.

More love, less hate.

The Five Important Things for Living a Successful and Fulfilling Life

There are five important things for living a successful and fulfilling life: never stop dreaming, never stop believing, never give up, never stop trying, and never stop learning.

When you open
your mind, you open
new doors to new
possibilities for yourself
and new opportunities
to help others.

Keep your mind open. The meaning of things lies in how people perceive them. The same thing could mean different meanings to the same people at different times.

Never let your mind
talk you out of your
dreams, trick you into
giving up. Never let
your mind become
the greatest obstacle
to success. To get your
mind on the right track,
the rest will follow.

Some things cannot be taught; they must be experienced. You never learn the most valuable lessons in life until you go through your own journey.

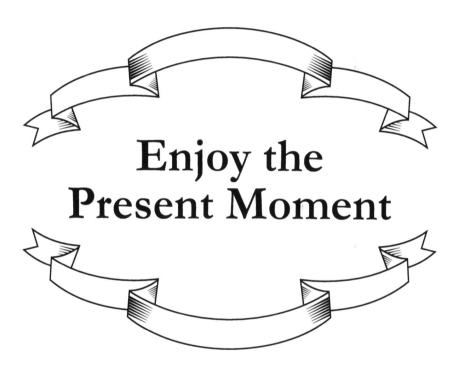

Enjoy the
Present Moment

Enjoy the Present Moment

If you want to be happy, do not dwell in the past, do not worry about the future, focus on living fully in the present. It is difficult to live in and enjoy the moment when you are thinking about the past or worrying about the future. You cannot change your past, but you can ruin the present by worrying about your future.

Learn from the past, plan for the future. The more you live in and enjoy the present moment, the happier you will be.

Do not set aside your happiness. Do not wait to be happy in the future. The best time to be happy is always now.

Happiness depends on your mindset and attitude.

You are in charge of your own happiness; you don't need to wait for other people's permission to be happy.

Don't waste your time in anger, regrets, worries, and grudges. Life is too short to be unhappy.

Never Put Happiness in Other People's Hands

Take responsibility of your own happiness; never put it in other people's hands.

Negative Thoughts
Make You Unhappy

Positive thoughts make you happy; negative thoughts make you unhappy. It's as simple as that. Your own thoughts are the only critical factor that makes you unhappy, and you can change them.

Nothing makes a person happier than having a happy heart.

Stop comparing yourself to other people, just choose to be happy and live your own life.

Perfectionism Is the Enemy of Happiness

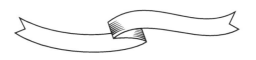

Perfectionism is the enemy of happiness. Embrace being perfectly imperfect. Learn from your mistakes and forgive yourself, you'll be happier. We make mistakes because we are imperfect. Learn from your mistakes, forgive yourself, and keep moving forward.

Smile more. Smiling can make you and others happy.

Do Not Lose
Your Smile

A smile puts you on the right track. A smile makes the world a beautiful place. When you lose your smile, you lose your way in the chaos of life.

Be the reason someone smiles. Be the reason someone feels loved and believes in the goodness in people.

Spend Your Life with People Who Make You Smile

Even if you cannot change all the people around you, you can change the people you choose to be around. Life is too short to waste your time on people who don't respect, appreciate, and value you. Spend your life with people who make you smile, laugh, and feel loved. It doesn't matter how many people you meet in your life; you just need the real ones who accept you for who you are and help you become who you should be.

No amount of regretting can change the past, and no amount of worrying can change the future. Nothing takes you away from dwelling in the past or worrying about the future like living in the present.

Inspirational Thoughts

Enthusiasm can help you find the new doors, but it takes passion to open them. If you have a strong purpose in life, you don't have to be pushed. Your passion will drive you there.

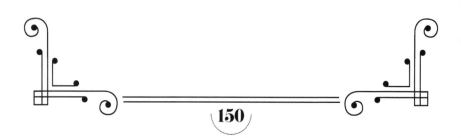

Achieve Greatness

No one has ever achieved greatness without dreams.

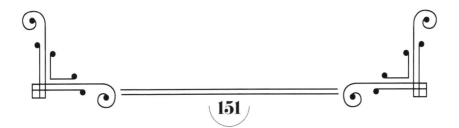

Take Actions

Dream big. Wake up. Take the first step into the unknown.

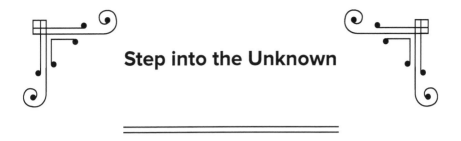

Until you step into the unknown, you don't know what you're made of.

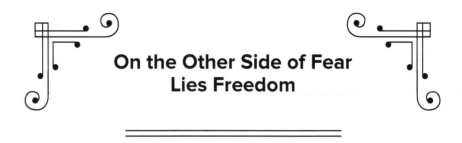

Growth always involves risk, and risk always involves fear. Fear robs you of your freedom to make the right choice in life that can bridge the gap between where you are and where you want to be. On the other side of fear, lies freedom. If you want to grow, you need to be brave and take risks. If you're not uncomfortable, you're not growing.

Courage is feeling fear, not getting rid of fear, and taking action in the face of fear.

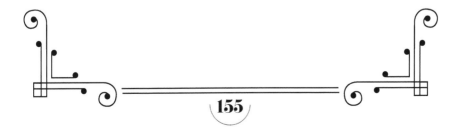

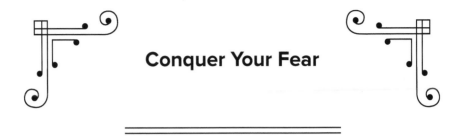

You have two choices, to conquer your fear or to let your fear conquer you.

To overcome fear is the quickest way to gain your self-confidence.

Never let fear hold you
captive.

Never let self-doubt hold
you captive.

Never let frustration hold
you captive.

Don't Wait for the Right Moment

Don't wait for the right moment to start, start and make each moment right.

The Time to Start

The beginning is always NOW.

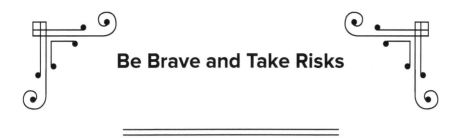

You need to have faith in yourself. Be brave and take risks. You don't have to have it all figured out to move forward.

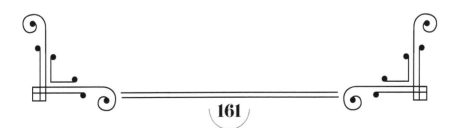

Don't wait for things to happen. Make them happen.

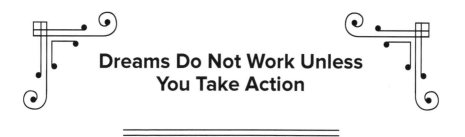

Dreams don't work unless you take action. The surest way to make your dreams come true is to live them.

Set goals to achieve your dreams. Take daily action that brings you closer to your goals. It doesn't matter how small that action is. Just take action.

**To Have What You Have
Never Had**

To have what you have
never had, you have to do
what you have never done.

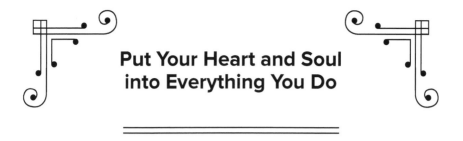

Put Your Heart and Soul into Everything You Do

You can have everything you want if you can put your heart and soul into everything you do.

**Do What You Love and
Love What You Do**

Do what you love,
love what you do, and
with all your heart give
yourself to it.

Do what is right, not what is easy nor what is popular.

Do What Is Right, Not What Is Easy

Stop doing what is easy or popular. Start doing what is right.

Do What Is Right

When you do the right thing, you get the feeling of peace and serenity associated with it. Do it again and again.

Never underestimate yourself when you do what is right. Never overestimate yourself when you do what is wrong.

What one thinks is right is not always the same as what others think is right; no one can be always right.

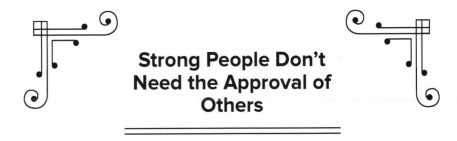

Strong People Don't Need the Approval of Others

Strong people have a strong sense of self-worth and self-awareness; they don't need the approval of others.

Great Things Happen in Your Life

Great things happen
to those who don't
stop believing, trying,
learning, and being
grateful.

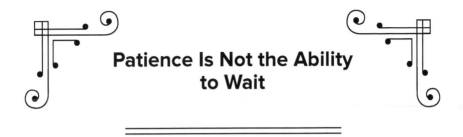
Patience is not the ability to wait. Patience is to be calm no matter what happens, constantly take action to turn it to positive growth opportunities, and have faith to believe that it will all work out in the end while you are waiting.

Top 15 Things Money Cannot Buy

- Time
- Happiness
- Inner Peace
- Integrity
- Love
- Character
- Manners
- Health
- Respect
- Morals
- Trust
- Patience
- Class
- Common sense
- Dignity

Don't Just

- Don't just learn, experience.
- Don't just read, absorb.
- Don't just change, transform.
- Don't just relate, advocate.
- Don't just promise, prove.
- Don't just criticize, encourage.
- Don't just think, ponder.
- Don't just take, give.
- Don't just see, feel.
- Don't just dream, do.
- Don't just hear, listen.
- Don't just talk, act.
- Don't just tell, show.
- Don't just exist, live.

Focus on your strengths, not your weaknesses.

Focus on your character, not your reputation.

Focus on your blessings, not your misfortunes.

Don't let your emotions get in the way of rational decision making.

Instead of complaining about the problem and blaming others, start finding the solution.

Nothing can disturb your peace of mind unless you allow it to.

Love People and Use Things

People were created to be loved and things to be used. The world becomes chaotic because things are being loved and people are being used. Most of us must learn to love people and use things rather than loving things and using people.

The Outer World Is a Reflection of the Inner World

The outer world is a reflection of the inner world. Other people's perception of you is a reflection of them; your response to them is an awareness of you.

Respect Other People's Feelings

Respect other people's feelings. It might mean nothing to you, but it could mean everything to them.

The Ultimate Form of Forgiveness

The ultimate form of forgiveness is in comprehending there's nothing to forgive.

You have to start doing something that makes you feel alive today, and then it could possibly evolve into something wonderful. Do something today.

Create your own miracles;
do what you think you
cannot do.

You have come a long way and have won many battles. Whenever you're faced with a difficult or challenging situation, you'll overcome it. Yes, you can.

Be where you are, stop over-thinking, and focus on what you are doing.

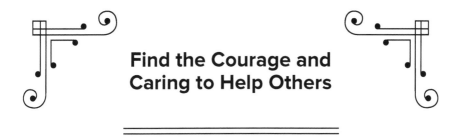

The strongest people find the courage and caring to help others, even if they are going through their own storm.

Be with someone who inspires you and makes you be the best version of yourself.

It takes guts and humility to admit mistakes. Admitting we're wrong is courage, not weakness.

Change How You Get Things Done

Until you change how you get things done, you'll never know what works best.

Try Something New

To learn something new, you need to try new things and not be afraid to be wrong. Find something that inspires you, dare to try something new; allow yourself to be open to whatever experience arises.

What's done is done. What's gone is gone. One of life's lessons is always moving on. It's okay to look back to see how far you've come but keep moving forward.

Don't let procrastination take over your life. Be brave and take risks. Your life is happening right now.

Everyone's time is limited. What matters most is to focus on what matters most.

Improve
Yourself

Improve Yourself

Let the improvement of yourself keep you so busy that you have no time to criticize others.

Make Improvements Not Excuses

Make improvements, not excuses. Seek respect, not attention.

Every new day is a new chance to improve your life—to grow happier, stronger, and wiser.

Stop comparing yourself to others. Always strive to improve yourself to become better today than you were yesterday to serve those around you and the world.

You learn something valuable from all of the significant events and people, but you never touch your true potential until you challenge yourself to go beyond imposed limitations.

It takes courage and wisdom to acknowledge there are areas where you could improve. Only in identifying your limitations can you stretch yourself beyond them.

Always believe in yourself and always stretch yourself beyond your limits. Your life is worth a lot more than you think because you are capable of accomplishing more than you know. You have more potential than you think, but you will never know your full potential unless you keep challenging yourself and pushing beyond your own self imposed limits.

There is no more profitable investment than investing in yourself. It is the best investment you can make; you can never go wrong with it. It is the true way to improve yourself to be the best version of you and lets you be able to best serve those around you.

Let go of something old that no longer serves you in order to make room for something new.

There's Always Room for Improvement

No matter how much experience you have, there's always something new you can learn and room for improvement.

Maturity is when you stop complaining and making excuses, and start making changes.

Maturity is when you stop complaining and making excuses in your life; you realize everything that happens in life is a result of the previous choice you've made and start making new choices to change your life.

You make the world a better place by making daily improvements to become the best version of yourself.

Goals and Success

Great goals make great people. People cannot hit what they do not aim for.

Cultivate the habit of setting clearly-defined written goals; they are the road maps that guide you to your destination.

Focus on your goals, not your fear. Focus like a laser beam on your goals.

Stay Focused

What you stay focused on will grow.

Failure Is a Part of Success

Failures are the stairs we climb to reach success.

Failure Is a Bend in the Road

Failure is a bend in the road, not the end of the road. Learn from failure and keep moving forward.

213

How much you can learn when you fail determines how far you will go into achieving your goals.

It doesn't matter how many times you get knocked down. All that matters is you get up one more time than you were knocked down.

The one who falls and gets up is stronger than the one who never tried. Do not fear failure but rather fear not trying.

Don't Give Up

When the going gets tough, put one foot in front of the other and just keep going. Don't give up.

---◆---

Stay strong, stay positive, and never give up.

Care about Something Enough

---◆---

If you care about something enough, you'll find a way to make it happen.

Don't Give Up

If you don't give up on something you truly believe in, you will find a way.

Don't Give Up

Change course, but don't give up.

Those who win never quit.

Those who quit never win.

Those who win never give up.

Those who give up never win.

What helps you persevere is your resilience and commitment.

Turn your obstacles into opportunities and your problems into possibilities.

222

People are successful
because they think and act
like successful people.

Successful people have no fear of failure. But unsuccessful people do. Successful people have the resilience to face up to failure—learn the lessons and adapt from it.

The level of success you achieve will be in direct proportion to the depth of your commitment.

---◆---

Do not rest on your laurels when you get to the top; you risk losing your edge once you let success go to your head.

Do not let arrogance go to your head and despair to your heart; do not let compliments go to your head and criticisms to your heart; do not let success go to your head and failure to your heart.

Listen with curiosity. Speak with honesty. Act with integrity. The greatest problem with communication is we don't listen to understand. We listen to reply. When we listen with curiosity, we don't listen with the intent to reply. We listen for what's behind the words.

Good leaders have vision and inspire others to help them turn vision into reality. Great leaders have vision, share vision, and inspire others to create their own. Great leaders create more leaders, not followers.

Great leaders can see the greatness in others when they can't see it themselves and lead them to their highest potential they don't even know.

Leaders are limited by their vision rather than by their abilities.

It's good to follow a good example, but it's better to always set a good example for others.

Stand Out

You were born to stand out, stop trying to fit in.

Integrity is doing what is right and truthful, and doing as you say you would do.

Integrity is doing the right thing when nobody's watching, and doing as you say you would do.

233

Consistency is the true foundation of trust. Either keep your promises or do not make them.

Keep your promises and be consistent. Be the kind of person others can trust. Never trust those who lie to you, and never lie to those who trust you.

When you encourage others, you boost their self-esteem, enhance their self-confidence, make them work harder, lift their spirits and make them successful in their endeavors. Encouragement goes straight to the heart and is always available. Be an encourager. Always.

Always remember people who have helped you along the way, and don't forget to lift someone up.

One of the best ways to influence people is to make them feel important. Most people enjoy those rare moments when others make them feel important. It is one of the deepest human desires.

7 Effective Ways to Make Others Feel Important

1. Use their name.

2. Express sincere gratitude.

3. Do more listening than talking.

4. Talk more about them than about you.

5. Be authentically interested.

6. Be sincere in your praise.

7. Show you care.

Do more listening than talking; talk more about them than about you. The more you talk about them, the more important they will feel. The more you listen to them, the more important you will make them feel.

A smart person knows how to talk. A wise person knows when to be silent. The wiser you get, the less you speak.

Be patient and open-minded in your interactions with others, find the positive attributes that they possess.

Shine your light and make a positive impact on the world; there is nothing so honorable as helping improve the lives of other.

Be the positive impact on the lives of others.

Make a Positive Difference in Someone's Life

Dedicate yourself to what gives your life true meaning and purpose; make a positive difference in someone's life.

Success is not how high you have climbed, but how you make a positive difference to the world.

What is your purpose in life?
How can you make your life more
meaningful? Are you living the
life of your dreams? How can you
make someone's life less difficult?
Dare to become what you are
capable of becoming. Be mindful.
Be grateful. Be positive. Be true. Be
kind. Success is not how high you
have climbed, but how you make a
positive difference to the world.

Printed in Great Britain
by Amazon